PENELOPE LEE

KEN PAINE ... Nowhere to Hide

Acknowledgements

My thanks to my partner, Ken Paine, for his willingness to share his story and his genius, for his patience and his humour throughout this project and for his enduring encouragement.

The creation of this book has been all consuming. The writing of it was a labour of love and the selection of paintings/photographs/drawings etc.. a joy. The intensely technical designing was more of a challenge and would have been completely beyond my capability. For our friend, Mahesh Patel, to volunteer to take over the responsibility for this was enormous. He has devoted hours and hours and hours to the task and both Ken and myself are most grateful and have valued the time we have been able to spend with him.I should also thank his long suffering family for loaning him to us during this period.

My thanks also to my friend, Tony Frazer Price, who was generous in lending his support. Being experienced in the publishing world, I valued his advice hugely.

Finally, my thanks to the authors and publishers from whose works I have quoted.

Most of the works included within this book are in private collections.

Copyright: Penelope Lee
Publisher: P M Korn
Designer: Mahesh Patel
Photographer: Jon Wyand
Printer: Grafo Industrias Graficas, Avda. Cervantes, 51 - Edif.21 - DENAC, 48970 Basauri (Vizcaya) SPAIN
ISBN: 978-0-9928072-0-7
First published: 2014

Penelope Lee

Dedication

For Ken …. with love

The content of this book is an accurate account of my life from my perspective and memory - Ken Paine 2013

Ken working on
'The Tree Feller'

Preface

'You can't manufacture dreams...WANT TO BET!'

Where does talent come from? Actually that's not a bad way to start this book. Where? Why? Who? Why? What? Why? Why? Why? Ken Paine never stops asking questions. Never stops enquiring and trying to find out. 'There's got to be a reason', he says. 'There has to be something more'.

So why me?

How is it that I am writing about the life, lives and loves of Ken Paine? Simply because I think I know him best, warts and all and there are a lot of them. I met Ken as a pupil when I went to him to learn and, years later, I am still with Ken, sharing his life and still learning. Eighty-seven years old is what he is now. That's an awful lot of living. Ken has spent his artistic life putting down the faces he has met along the way. Faces from all walks of life and many cultures. Crammed into those eighty-seven years is a life that is as extraordinary as it is unique. Actually, I hate the misuse of the word unique and therefore I won't use it of Ken .

.....I'll stick with extraordinary.

The beauty of Ken is that both he and his life have been and continue to be extraordinary. I believe that his talent is the outcome of his life's journey - unusual and varied, full of love, hurt and passion - all of which he brings to his work, turning the one dimensional into three dimensional. With the twist of a head, the glint of an eye, he lets you know more about the sitter than you would ever glean from most portraits. He paints with zest and emotion. His paintings sing and convey. Ken is a master and through my time with him, I have listened, questioned and travelled through much of his life - unusual by any yardstick. We have talked about so many aspects of his history that perhaps I can claim to be qualified to give a three dimensional view of the man, the painter and the fascinating person that is .

.. Ken Paine.

Overleaf: 'The Ambassador of Shanty Town'

Lambeth 1926 - 1937

'Bantam Weight' - an early pastel
Won a few; lost a lot. Ken Paine

Although I did mention the word 'discipline' in a previous paragraph, that isn't a word that can readily be ascribed to Ken. In many ways he was always a little wild boy. Lambeth was such a place in those days. Such a wonderful, cosmopolitan, extreme sort of place. Aunt Louise's house, 1 Paris Street (later the numbering changed and it became 36 Paris Street) had been one of a row in row after row of houses stretching back from the river to The Cut – the heart of Lambeth.

At one end of The Cut was a boxing ring; there were stalls all along with pubs, Jewish bakers, tailors and pawnbrokers, shops selling jellied eels, fish and chips, pie and liquor, faggots and pease pudding. There were street performers – escape-ologists and jugglers and suchlike. There was fighting in the streets and much laughter and drunken revelry, all lit by gaslight turned on and off by a man with a big bamboo pole. The light was inadequate by today's standards but cast exaggerated and dramatic shadows, highlighting features in a fashion that started to shape Ken's perception and portraiture of the future.

As an aside, Ken remembers that his father remained in awe of electric light to the day he died. He would stand in the doorway and flick the switch and say to Ken ' just look at that son' and Ken, bemused, would look and say … 'Yeah. So?'

The brightest parts of Lambeth were the Lambeth Walk, The Cut, Waterloo Station, the Old Vic, Blackfriars Boxing Ring and the cinemas – the Gatti's and the Ideal Music Hall. Ken's overall memory does, perhaps, have a romantic slant but specifically he remembers …..

His grandmother, his mother's mother, Granny 'emmings, living in one of the Peabody Buildings*, with a heart as big as they come and a personality full of fun. Her fridge was a piece of string hanging out of the window and her water supply was a shared one on the landing. He remembers her giving him sixpence carefully wrapped up and put in the palm of his hand and being sent along to the pub on the corner for the landlord to fill Granny 'emmings' chamber pot with Guinness. He remembers running wild with his friends causing mischief and mayhem: lighting fires in the alleyways; stealing cakes from the baker; fighting with gangs from rival streets; following the horses and carts and jumping on the back for rides. 'Whip behind Govn'r', the watching pedestrians would shout. The drunks with their caps and scarves and red bloated faces and the women on their doorsteps, breast feeding their babies and keeping an eye on the kids whilst chatting and gossiping with the neighbours.

It is all gone now. All knocked down in favour of high rise blocks. All that comraderie lost. Families today may have electric light and heat, they may have television and computers, they may be well fed …. but something was lost. Probably it is down to the sheer number of people today but human nature is vulnerable to its surroundings.

White scarves tied in a knot and a cap pulled over one eye were the fashion of the streets. Kids often used to wear each other's clothes and sometimes a boy would even have to go to school in his sister's clothes because they were the only ones available. Clothes were washed and dried the same night for putting back on.

---

* The Peabody Trust was founded by an American philanthropist, George Peabody, who was so shocked by the squalid living conditions in the slums of the capital that, in 1862, he gifted $2.5 million to create homes with the basic essentials to relieve the hardship of poor Londoners. There is a statue of George Peabody in Threadneedle Street in the City.

'The Christian'
Hell & Damnation - I
did this at 3.00 o'clock
in the morning. It was
created out of my
head - there must be a
reason?
Ken Paine

The kids would play football in the street with a ball made of wet paper crushed like papier-mache and tied up with string. It didn't have any bounce but it did a job. Wickets were chalked on to the wall and cricket was played with a homemade bat and a ball made of sorbot which was often more square than round with great chunks missing. There was a fizzy drinks' lorry that would come around the streets and the children would go out with their jugs to be filled. The organ grinder, who came along with his little merry-go-round that you could go on in exchange for any empty glass jars.

The kids would suck gobstoppers, those giant marble type everlasting sweets, and pass them around to each other so they all had a suck. And Ken and his mates would invest in a tin of condensed milk and sit in a circle greedily spooning it into their mouths until it was all gone.

The streets stank, the only pleasant smells being from the food cooking but the drains were poor.

There was no authorised betting in those days and it was done by runners taking money off the corner of the street. The police would chase the runners — sometimes even over the tops of houses and, ever the artist, Ken retains a clear picture of those silhouettes against the evening sky.

Opposite: 'Port & Lemon'

'Port & lemon'' a resident of Peabody Buildings, Blackfriars

There is a school of thought that you should not try and explain a painting but let it talk for itself. One, actually, that I adhere to.

But I love, love, love this painting and I want to share my feelings about it. I'm not the artist, so perhaps that is allowed. Maybe, some of you who are unfamiliar with this Ken Paine style will be baffled. It is so loose and seemingly careless and yet it epitomises everything Ken seeks to achieve. Emotion. A feeling. A reaction to one of his characters. Characters he doesn't want the world to forget.

This gloriously ugly, aging lady sitting in a pub that probably has sticky tables and an over-patterned grubby carpet, bad lighting, yellowing ceilings and a loo that smells of disinfectant with a lock that doesn't always work. There she is in her well worn hat looking vacant but missing nothing and nursing her port & lemon, her favoured tipple. Her hands are gnarled and have known a lifetime of hard work, are probably arthritic and unreliable. She's been coming to this pub all her life. She's never been anywhere and grew up locally. She's seen things change, the piano that used to be the life and soul has either gone or been abandoned in the corner. Her youth likewise. The pub probably has been decorated and sometimes even cleaned but fundamentally nothing has changed. This is her place, her night out. This is where she comes and sits and looks and drinks her drink. Others have come and gone and maybe she does little more than nod to the odd acquaintance but all the same, it's her place.

All this. This is what this painting gives me.

The church and its disciples would walk down Maxwell Street at one end of The Cut, trying to convert the ungodly but nobody took much notice. The kids would try to set fire to their robes as they passed by. Ken would be taken along to Christ Church in Lambeth to see the nit nurse along with most of the other children he mixed with. The nurse would drag a fine toothed metal comb through his hair until there was no further sign of the nits but leaving his scalp bleeding.

The children would run alongside an ambulance shouting 'touch collar, never swolla, never catch the fever'. In fact Ken's whole childhood was beset with superstition. He was brought up to believe that if he looked in the mirror for more than five minutes, he would see the devil. And the seeds of his hypochondria were sown in those early years by a father who constantly worried about germs.

Always up to mischief, Ken remembers playing in and around the buildings of St Thomas's Hospital. On one occasion, he had been playing with a friend, tiptoeing his way around the edge of a huge oil tank. He slipped and found himself up to his neck in oil. Only because of his upper body strength was he able to drag himself up out of the cloying liquid. His mate, terrified, had run off. Too frightened to go home in that state Ken went to the park and tried to clean himself with leaves.

In 1935, when the coaches brought the supporters down from West Bromich Albion and Sheffield Wednesday to Wembley for the FA Cup Final, he remembers chasing alongside with all the other children, shouting … 'throw out your mouldies'. The 'mouldies' in question being halfpennies and farthings. In November 1936, when he was ten years old, Ken remembers seeing the sky lit up and the smoke from the fire that burned down Crystal Palace. And he remembers some of the Jarrow marchers knocking on his Aunt's door.

Saturday was his favourite day. The day he got to go to the pictures. The very core of his life. The films. He would be given an orange and a bag of nuts to go in with for the price of his ticket, one penny and the cinema would always be partially filled with tramps keeping warm. Attendants would walk down the rows with a disinfectant spray to kill the fleas. Sometimes he used to get in without paying. One of the boys paid and then opened the back door and the rest would sneak in. The audience would be watching the screen and see the outline of six or seven kids creeping across.

Saturday was the day he could lose himself in the fantasies portrayed. There were serials every week, such as 'The Undersea Kingdom' and the boys would pile out after the film and pick up bits and pieces of wood and emulate the sword fights they had just been watching. It was also the day he could buy his secondhand comics: 'The Funny Wonder'; 'The Hotspur'; 'Film Fun'. along with their stains and creases ready to pore over later on. He would be sent to the fish & chip shop, 'Old Lou's', to get his tea, faggots and pease pudding, in his bowl. And then run home in the dark, along the musty alleyway, jumping over the step "where the dead woman was" racing back to Aunt Louise, who would pop his tea in the range and fill the tub for his bath. After that he would happily eat his tea and read his comics before bed at 6.30 pm, when he climbed the stairs with his candle to the top of the house complete with a mad lodger. He would lie in bed, not ready to sleep, squashing the bugs that had crawled out of the horsehair mattress.

Sunday was different. It was quiet and more formal and there were winkles for tea with bread and butter. Ken, ever aware of his stomach, would complain that there wasn't enough to eat but he would pick out the winkles from their shells with a pin and laugh with his family when they used the little caps as beauty spots.

His sister, Iris, was a different kettle of fish. Seven years older than Ken with memories of her mother and the show-biz lifestyle that went with it, she struggled to come to terms with her altered life with Aunt Louise. She was wild, hampered with less intelligence and, to be fair, less education than Ken and full of anger. Iris found learning difficult and couldn't read until very late in her youth. In many ways she was a vicious little termagant. I remember saying to Ken once, when he was describing Iris tap-dancing on table tops with ribbons on her shoes, that she must have been very cute being so tiny and talented. 'No' he reacted instantly, 'she was a bitch and used to fight in the street with razors.' As quickly as one image forms in your head, it is replaced by another, much darker, one. These little bits and pieces that sometimes come up surely offer a very true and real insight into his life, for a brief moment stripping him of his romance and laying him bare. Ken remembers his Dad having to pick her up and drag her home after that particular incident.

Iris also had to take on some of the responsibility of raising Ken, something she resented but then, she was only a child herself. On one, never to be forgotten occasion, she took him out to Archbishop's Park and put him in the swing for babies and toddlers .... and then wandered off and forgot about him. When Albert came home at 7 o'clock and asked where her brother was, she finally remembered. Bert had to race to the park, which was shut, and climb over the fence to rescue poor little Ken who was still there, swinging back and forth. It was pitch black and cold and very, very lonely. But Iris was sharp in other ways. One of her jobs later on, was delivering hats in the West End ...on roller skates!

The West End. That pinnacle of opulence. Just over the other side of Westminster Bridge - a positive citadel juxtaposed to the dark and dingy streets of Lambeth. Ken and his mates would follow the top hats walking over Westminster Bridge, pick up the dogends and have a quick puff.

The sound of Big Ben would resonate over the whole scene.

- oOo -

The faces of Lambeth have stayed with Ken and form the basis of a number of his paintings. His own family ... the posh side and ... the not so posh side. The women sitting on their doorsteps in Lambeth breastfeeding their children. The grubby schoolchildren running around with their socks round their ankles and their threadbare coats. The Jewish traders, the tough working men and the boxers. The warmth and humour in the faces as well as the dread and despair. A pretty powerful springboard to a career of painting faces

And, of course, he has never lost the accent. Floor is flauwa; door is dauwa; across is across't and so on and so forth. His father who had benefited from a good education himself, used to despair but that was the environment into which he put Iris and Ken.

'Clean Shirt Day'

'To look is to listen.'

The Thames

That mighty river has been a constant in Ken's life. There was the initial division of rich and poor, light and dark if you like. There are memories of swimming with his friends at Vauxhall, diving off the barges in amongst the debris gathered at the edge. The dead rats and the filthy detritus that was a consequence of a working river in those days. No wonder he developed diphtheria at the age of seven years. He once found a brass knuckle-duster at the foot of Lambeth Bridge, obviously thrown over the side in a moment of panic.

Later, in the 1940s, he would walk along the banks of the river, courting his latest love in the shadows of the Victorian water fountain in Twickenham, witnessed the severe winters when the river iced over and remembers his friend Eddie's parents having a market stall on the ice. He remembers the diver (Cockles) who used to walk under water with a homemade helmet on his head. Eel Pie Island, which was later made famous by the Rolling Stones, and where he met and lunched with Trevor Bayliss the inventor of the windup radio,

to whom he was introduced by his very good friend, Sir Alec Reed, a long standing supporter and a great humanitarian.

In Lambeth he had an uncle, one of his father's brothers, who used to swim across the Thames in his lunch hour; another who would sleep walk along the Embankment and be seen safely home by the local coppers. And later, much later in the mid 1990s, he had a studio on Platt's Ayot on the Thames at Lower Sunbury, a wonderful sanctuary full of the flotsam and jetsam of life. Musicians, hippies, boat-builders, speculators, small businesses; a full working music studio; a business selling bits and pieces acquired abroad, useless nothings such as artificial rocks that could be lit up and models of black jazz musicians — you know the kind of thing. But great people. There were some young men who were growing cannabis in greenhouses — supposedly some sort of experimental farming business seeking to feed the overpopulated world! Strangely they disappeared overnight. There were the boat-builders and the boathouse builders. There

was a café and a caravan selling coffee and bacon butties and then there was Ken Paine's studio.

It was on this shambolic island full of derelict machinery and decrepit boathouses that Ken taught his students. On they staggered once a week across the bridge burdened with easels and canvasses and paints. Dressed expensively and shod ridiculously, with painted nails and bohemic aspirations. They would paint and learn and laugh and at lunchtime they would adorn a tatty old pasting table with cloth and candelabra and sit with their wine and delicacies whilst being ogled by the locals. A halcyon period for all really and, perhaps more importantly, some good art came out of it and some good artists grew better.

But that is leaping ahead. Ken led several lives before then.

'After the Storm'

'Nowhere to go'

'The House Master'
Warts and all - probably how the pupils see him. Ken Paine

for all his love of films and all his romanticism didn't want to know. He needed his own life and his own adventure.

This independent adventuring spirit started to exert itself at about this time, when Ken was 13. He went with a local gypsy family to Kent, hop-picking. He remembers that they all slept in a wooden box-like structure in the middle of the field, sleeping on the straw strewn floor. During the day they all worked, picking the hops. After about three days, Ken had had enough and decided to go home. He had no ticket for the journey but bought himself a platform ticket (these allowed access to the platform for the price of one penny). He, however, got on the train to Waterloo and spent most of the journey in the lavatory hiding from the ticket collector. He also remembers that there was a large number of cockneys on the train and that they had stolen a baby pig from the farm they had been working on, which spent most of the journey squealing. When he got home, his Dad was astonished at the dark colour that the sun had turned his young son, who was proudly showing off his body in a tight-fitting string vest.

A couple of years later, at the age of 15, Ken went to Southampton with a mate to try and get on a ship as a cabin boy. He actually managed to get on the ship at the docks but then someone came along and said they had a full crew and couldn't take any more. The two friends were turned off the boat and stayed in a hostel in Southampton, which he thinks was free, one person, one partition with a bed. He doesn't remember that he even told his father where he was going

Actually, thinking about it, perhaps these two examples weren't the first demonstrations of his adventuring spirit because, when he was a much younger boy, he would entrance his schoolyard friends with his plans to take off to somewhere new. He persuaded them all to arrange to meet on Waterloo Bridge the next morning, early. Ken was there

but nobody else turned up and he was left on the bridge with his corned beef sandwich carefully wrapped up and had to go back home and dream and plan something else. You see, Ken's dreams were real to him. They weren't playtime games, they were real plans. They still are..

In those early war years, Ken felt he had the world to himself. He was strong and fit and handsome. His nickname was Tarzan because he was so physical and always climbing trees. The girls liked him and he liked them. They would sneak out of their houses and bring him cigarettes they had nicked from their fathers. They would wait for him outside his house and Iris would lean out of the window and shout … 'he doesn't wash his neck, you know'.

His friend, Eddie, would join him in his adventures.

Eddie, Edgar, was some four or five years younger than Ken and Ken always thought of him as his 'little mate'. They shared a large part of their childhood and Eddie was important to Ken and deserves this passage in the book.

Even as a child, Eddie was a depressive and would sit staring out of the window. His mother would sometimes give Ken half a crown and beg him to take him out. He tried to emulate Ken, whom he adored and called 'Tarzan'. He would climb trees, swinging on the branches. But he simply wasn't built the same way and, predictably, fell and broke his leg. Ken had to carry him home on his back.

They would swim together in the Thames. Changing on the barges where Eddie would wrap a bit of sheet around himself to preserve his modesty, little realising that when he emerged from the water the sheet clung to him accentuating the very thing(s) he was seeking to hide! His young friend grew into an awkward unhappy man but he adored Ken and later proved himself to be

Ken and Eddie 1986

something of a Tarzan in his own way. Ken retains a great deal of respect for the man. He wasn't blessed with many assets and yet he took on the world bravely.

Much later, when they were adults, Ken and Eddie came across each other again. Ed couldn't paint very well but he tried and Ken gave him a few tips and found him a job doing quick sketches in a strip joint in Soho. Sometimes, the pundits would request that he sketched the showgirls. He was often, sadly, the object of other people's fun and they would watch him work and say …. 'give 'em a bit more tit, Ed'.

One day he decided he wanted an adventure of his own. Ken had regaled him with the stories of his travels and Eddie put an easel on his back, dressed himself in a sheet and took himself off to Italy. He walked the length and breadth of the country, moving on to France, sketching to pay for his food before getting inadvertently embroiled in an affair involving the Mafia. He was shot in the face with pellets from a shotgun and was wrongly imprisoned, only saving himself from disaster by adopting the role of prison tattooist. The role kept him safe from fellow inmates. But he had hard lessons to learn, not least, at his first meal when his food was served into his hand. He had no receptacle and had to scrounge an old tin can for future meals.

One day, back home, Ken read in the paper that an Englishman, Edgar Raymond, was in trouble, had been beaten and was in hospital. He tried to find him and bring him home. He went to France, grape-picking his way around, sleeping in a burnt out car, but everywhere he went and asked about his friend, he seemed to have just missed him. By now, Eddie was penniless. His easel had been smashed by a group of youths and he was surviving on Beetle Nuts from the fields. He became very ill. He finally got in touch with Ken who sent him the money for his fare home.

When he died, Ken was given one or two of his possessions, one being a small black book with telephone numbers and a couple of sketches in. At the back, in his fairly illiterate hand, Eddie had written …. 'my best friend – Ken Paine'.

'Whisky' The worst sitter I've ever had, such a nosey cat. Ken Paine

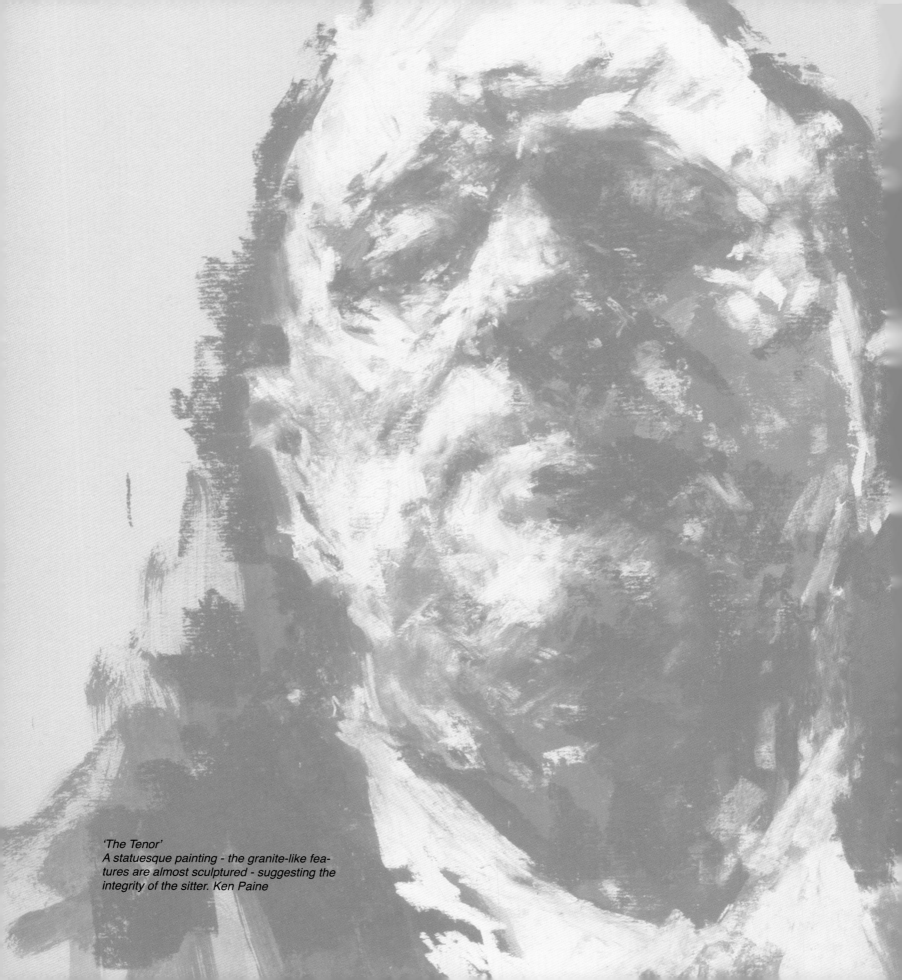

'The Tenor'
A statuesque painting - the granite-like features are almost sculptured - suggesting the integrity of the sitter. Ken Paine

'Spontaneous Values'
Ken Paine

that way. He'll intend to do something but be immediately and completely distracted by something, anything, that crosses his horizon.

- oOo -

Ken and his mob (the Queen's) were sent over to Ireland to help handle the surrender of the German U Boats at Lizerharle. He spent about two and a half years in Ireland all in, all over. His stories are vague and mixed. He remembers guarding the prisoners but more in the way of hanging out with them and sharing the odd fag. One of the prisoners made him a cigarette box inset with his boxing medal. He remembers one of his colleagues, bored and on watch urging him to leave the gate open ... so he could enjoy shooting those trying to escape! (He declined). He remembers a bit of smuggling. Rowing over the bay to Donegal in Southern Ireland for radios and booze. He remembers flogging blankets to the locals in the Mountains of Mourne.... I wonder where he got those from? He remembers gathering and eating Whelks on the shore. He remembers ransacking the U Boats for tins of strawberry jam whilst the intelligent ones, took souvenirs/valuables, brass instruments and suchlike. He remembers the boats beings used for torpedo practice off shore until they were all sunk.

He remembers some of the kids in Londonderry following him and the other soldiers around, holding out their hands and begging .... 'Gi'us a penny mister'. They would be pale and their skinny frames were exaggerated by the fact they often wore their dad's old jackets. He remembers one woman dragging him into her house to get him off the streets and out of the way because of a danger from the IRA. She probably saved his life. He remembers the women ... naturally.

Believe me, all these faces are in his paintings. A life of observation and a wealth of material to draw on.

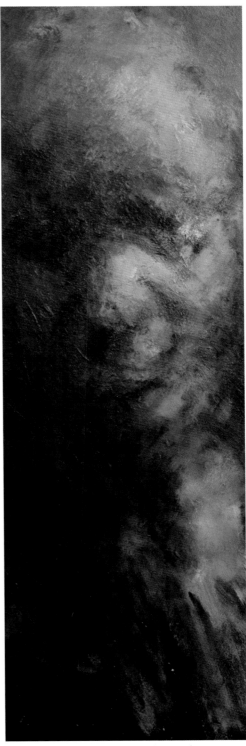

'Underneath the Arches'

His trips home on leave were long awaited and desperately disappointing. The change of life away from home and independence had altered everything. Like so many found after the war, it was impossible to go back.

75

"L'enfant"

'Youth'

'The coal was full of shit and slate.
That's what fucked the 4 – 8.
The 8 – 12 went down like men
But they were fucked by half past 10.
The 12 – 4 could do no more
So they packed their gear and went ashore.

Davey Jones needs another trimmer'

The Merchant Navy

So once he was de-mobbed, Ken joined the Merchant Navy. It wasn't so much a career choice as an opportunity. Ever the 'chancer', Ken went off to Newcastle in 1948 to train to be a Stoker (or Fireman, as they were then known). The training was not what you could call technical or intense. Once he had learned to chuck a shovel load of coal into a moving barrel he was considered ready. Oh, and he had to have his tonsils removed for some unknown reason. He signed on to 'The Ravens Point' at the London Docks in February 1949. £14.00 a month all found.

So began a life of travel, adventure and growing. The work was hard. Back breaking and soul-destroying for many. But for Ken, with a body like a wrestler and a thirst for life, it was freedom. A stoker on those old steam ships worked a four-hour shift, eight hours off and then over and over again. Even then, his artistic ability was apparent. After each shift, the stoker finishing would write a message or draw a cartoon or picture on the bulkhead in chalk for the next shift. Ken's offerings stood out a mile.

There were usually two stokers working each shift, each responsible for three fires and they had to keep them like that or the ship would ... stop. It was hot, it was physical and it was draining. They would come out of the coal hole, black and sweaty and go up on deck to wash down in cold water. Each fire was the size of a small room and the ash and clinker had to be cleared and raked with a great paddle balanced on the shoulder and moved 'to and fro'; the coal would be shovelled into the fires and air introduced to keep them blazing. The ash and clinker had to be heaved up on deck with a strong arm (pulley) and tipped over the side. And if it caught the wind, it would blow straight back into your face. To begin with Ken's whole body hurt and he was amongst rough, tough, often ignorant men. He had to have his wits about him and could rarely rest. He often says that his 'slitty' eyes helped him in those days because nobody could tell if he was asleep or awake. Later, he worked as a stoker on oil burners, which was a soft option in comparison. He was on the Queen Mary on more than one occasion, where he had excellent food and comfortable accommodation. Unlike those early days, when he had to fill his own palliasse with straw from the dockside. As Ken says ... 'they had sheets and everything!'

On his first trip, well aware of his youth and the hard men he would be mixing with, he gave himself up to his imagination gleaned from the films. He put on his gear, carried a large suitcase

'Not so Simple Simon'

joke with him that 'old Hogarth has been knocking on the wall all night waiting for you and your sketchbook'. In fact it wasn't a sketchbook, but a pile of pink paper that he worked on. Pink because that was the cheapest available.

Sadly the old House in which they were living was being renovated and the family had to find somewhere else to live. They moved into a pre-fab. To the uninitiated, one of those emergency homes erected en masse after the war to cope with the desperate housing shortage. Never meant to last, they were constructed of tin and had two bedrooms, a lounge, kitchen and bathroom with a tiny garden. Ken liked it and despite their intended short life, there are still some pre-fabs in use today.

Ken's interest in art was coming more to the fore. He would take himself off to the library after work and look up the art books. Studying the masters, Valazquez, Rembrandt, Goya. All the greats in fact but those three, perhaps, being the biggest draw and fascination. He would look and look and learn to understand their techniques. The old library in Chiswick was a favourite haunt and he would sit in that lovely old building in the peace and quiet and devour his books. To this day, Ken will still spend his spare time in the library looking up and learning new things – mostly medical and has worked his way through many tomes. He is very knowledgeable about illnesses and diseases, disastrously so as he is a self-confessed hypochondriac.

He comes from a generation that is comfortable with books. He enjoys books, the feel of them and the look of them. It seems so sad that, that touch with paper is lost on today's youth, who find what they want from the internet. No doubt it is more efficient but somehow it is efficient without feeling. Like a modern, minimilistic, building that you are frightened to sit down in, in case you make it look messy. Still, you don't miss what you have never had and maybe this generation will one day regret the passing of the keyboard.

'Reflection'

'The Crusader'

'Reminiscing'

'Where do you start and where do you end?'

America … again

Off-season Ken would be drawn back to America. Blue couldn't understand it. He was gaining a reputation as an artist. His work was being shown in the Portrait Society exhibitions. She felt he should concentrate and build on that. But he would travel over to San Francisco on his own looking for experience and work. He was armed with a letter of introduction from T H Rowney of George Rowney & Co., to assist with his requirements of art supplies. Ken had got to know Rowney, because of his large purchases of pastels and paper and found him a likeable and inter-

esting character. Rowney had travelled America himself selling his wares to the various retail outlets. Later Ken met up with him again, just off the Tottenham Court Road in London, for high tea with Sir William Russell Flint RA.

Ken has crossed paths with many great artists in his time and once sat opposite Augustus John on the tube in London. He said he was an old man by then and what he remembered most was his 'starey' eyes. He was a formidable (looking) character. He used to see Stanley Spencer at the London

Ken and friends with the artist Terence Cuneo at an art exhibition

Terence Cuneo

112

'Resident of San Francisco'

A cheeky photograph of Ken and friend in the early sixties

dockside in his Merchant Navy days. And he painted a portrait of the artist, Terence Cuneo OBE (the official artist for the Coronation painting for Queen Elizabeth II in 1953) just weeks before his death in 1996.

In San Francisco, Ken put on a suit and a sober expression and took himself off to Macy's where he sold them the idea that they needed him. He said with his frightfully (frightful) English accent that he was an artist of some repute and could work in their furniture department as an adviser, selling the customer an appropriate piece of artwork to go with their new furniture. And they bought it! They hired him and he made them money But that job went the way of them all. He ended up being shown the door. The Manager had come to work to find Ken and his fellow workers playing jazz and jiving around the store.

Even then he managed to hang on until after Christmas by telling the manager that he would, of course, go but that he (the manager) would have to disappoint the boss's daughter whom he had promised to paint. He hadn't but he was paid up to the New Year.

Seeking fellow artists and all things artistic, Ken looked up the directory to find out where the art shops were. He drifted towards them and found himself in the right part of town. He visited a gallery where he fell into conversation with a handsome black man, Burton E Moore. Discovering that each was an artist, the guy offered Ken some wall space and an opportunity to paint portraits on the corner of Colombo and Broadway. It wasn't long before Ken realised that the building housed living accommodation at the back and was used to run a sideline of prostitutes. Under the counter in the front of shop was a loaded gun.

Having been raised in the way he had been and having been in the company of the friends of Iris as a boy, Ken took it all in his stride. Didn't, in fact, turn a hair. Rather embraced the whole as a new experience. Burton E was a pimp but he was a good guy (if that is not an oxymoron), intelligent and talented. He would dress himself in a leotard and waltz out on the streets leading an ocelot with a diamond studded collar. Or his Afghan hound that he would berate for being stuck up. He would always call Ken 'Mr Paine' and described him as 'a knave'. When they went out to the restaurants and jazz clubs together, Ken would paint his portraits at the back. Burton E would tell the gathering crowds to just wait and watch and the image would appear. He

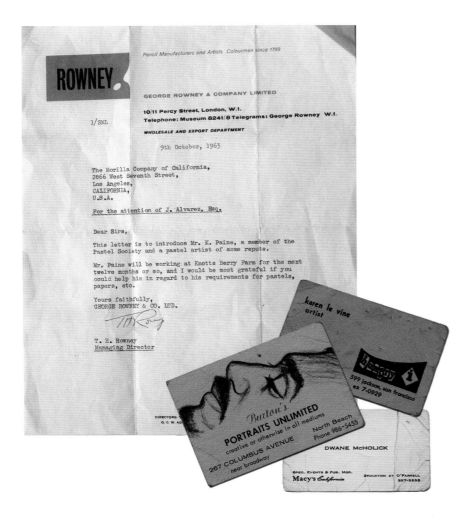

Letter of introduction given to Ken by T H Rowney of George Rowney & Co Ltd and the three business cards are from his time in San Francisco. The 'Hungry i' was a jazz club

Overleaf: 'The Decision'

had a lot of respect for Ken the artist and held him in some awe. And that was how Ken always painted. He would work his wonderful shapes and the faces would appear. No outline, No discernible features until, quite suddenly, you realise there is face on the canvas.

A colourful and over the top lifestyle and yet of its time. The hippies would gather at Height Asprey and the whole mix was heady and loose. No longer a teenager or even in his twenties, Ken did however take full advantage of the age.

Together Ken and Burton E ran a topless shoeshine business. The girls would be adorned with nothing on their top other than tassles on their breasts and would kneel to clean the shoes and boots of the passing punters.

It was a laugh. It was a freedom and Ken embraced it all. He found time to paint and he had admirers of his work wherever he went.

But yet again there is a reality that must be understood. Hunger at times to a degree where Ken would learn the tricks of the trade and pick up the crackers given away free in cafés and restaurants and the ketchup which he would mix with boiling water to make soup. To this day he will always put an extra sachet of sugar in his pocket in a café …. after all, you never know?

Ever exploring, he had a desire to experiment with time and financially embarrassed, he housed himself in the only apartment he could afford, a basement flat with black walls. He couldn't see the sky outside the windows and he incarcerated himself and timed how long it took him to make a cup of tea. Some days later he timed himself again doing the same task. Time had ceased to have any meaning and he was working in slow motion. He got a bit frightened and took himself off to an all night diner for some ham and eggs. Today he is a fan of the American artist Edward Hopper. He can relate to the loneliness portrayed in those empty diners and landscapes.

'Worrying is just meditation for realists.'

Norah, Ken and John

Divorce - 1966

Sadly his marriage was under considerable strain and it became obvious that Ken and Blue were no longer the same people who had married so urgently so young. Blue was from a naval family and, as she said, she had married a young stoker .... not an artist. Ken was most definitely now an artist and his reputation and prowess was growing. He was beginning to be noticed. He was moving in circles where he met other artists and he loved it. He found it inspiring and exhilarating. It was what he was meant to be but, in truth, it didn't really include a family.

The pair had grown up in different ways and, by the time they divorced, there were many secrets and lies. However right or obvious the decision, there is always a lot of associated pain. Ken left Blue his business in the camps but she was hurt and furious. She raged at the unfairness of it all. The kids were 15 and 16 respectively.

Blue later remarried and that marriage has lasted some forty years but to this day, she has not forgiven him and is absolutely determined to outlive 'the bastard'. I have never heard Ken speak ill of her.

Ken is hugely proud of his two children. Despite everything, his daughter, Norah, grew up to be an extremely successful business woman in Australia where she still lives today surrounded by her children and grandchildren. His son, John, is a very knowledgeable and successful Antique Dealer and lives with his wife in Hampshire. They too have a son.

Overleaf: 'Of One Accord'

A Marvellous Portraitist!

His works showed at the International Salon of Lille (France) attracted immediately the admiration of each visitor. Doubtless Ken PAINE is a portraitist 'out of banality' as we meet too few in a generation. The 'REMBRANDT' of Pastel Painting, that was the hearty cry of many visitors of the Salon. His paintings full of strength , are resulting of a subtle and deep observation.

Those who were lucky to see Ken PAINE working were amazed, he does not paint: he sculptures, models his subjects with all his fingers, without stopping to examine him. Ken PAINE does not seem to take himself seriously, he is painting seriously, that's all. He gives us a great lesson of humility. Full of experiences (that's showed on his clear cut face) he is always kind and gentle. When he releases you, a friend is missing.

Janine MORVILLIER

'People don't give you dreams, you make your own.'

Moving on - 1990s

At home, Ken's relationship with his girl-friend broke down. They had shared a happy and eventful time together and their friendship remains strong. Jill bought a flat in Twickenham and moved on to find another life.

His daughter was by now living indepen-dently and he formed a new relationship with a fellow artist, Debra Manifold.

Yet again Debra was young, just 29 when they met. She was an aspiring artist with an art school education and a working background in the media. When she met Ken, she was working for the Linda Blackstone Gallery and, through Debra, Ken began a long association with Linda Blackstone. In 1997, he trav-elled with Linda, Debra and a group of fellow artists to Israel.

"Renowned for his highly charged indi-vidualistic, characterful portraits, Ken Paine filled three large sketchbooks during the twelve-day trip and recalls 'from the moment we stepped off the plane at Tel Aviv, 'I had the feeling of some biblical adventure about to take place. It was the people both Jews and

Ken and Debra

'Into the Light of Day'

Arabs, that filled me with a great artistic urge to paint and record.'

In his youth Paine was addicted to drawing and whilst he received some training at Twickenham Art College, he was primarily self-taught. Late in 1944 he joined the Queen's Royal Regiment and four years later, after his demob, joined the Merchant Navy which brought periods working on the Queen Elizabeth and the Queen Mary. Many of his voyages took him to New York, where the characters of the deprived areas of Harlem, Queens and Brooklyn became a source for his pictures.

His first solo show came in 1963 at the Gough Brothers Gallery and shortly after he had three works accepted for inclusion in the Pastel Society's annual exhibition. Since then he has shown regularly at the Society and in 1982 was elected a member. In London his work has become a well-known feature of the annual shows of the Royal Society of Portrait Painters, The Royal Institute of Painters in Water Colours and the Royal Institute of Oil Painters. Solo shows have included the Hampton Hill Gallery and the Llewellyn Alexander Gallery.

Although Paine does paint to commission and his sitters have included Sir David Stern and the newsreader Trevor McDonald, he has always had an unquenchable fascination with faces that tell a story. A painter of social reality, his shrewdly observed subjects are frequently aged and often street down-and-outs or gypsies. His models are often found in pubs and in less salubrious venues, such as Lambeth's notorious 'Cardboard City'.

'Antique Collecting' – April 1998 (Linda Blackstone Gallery of Pinner in association with the Jewish National Fund, Israel's equivalent of the British National Trust, arranged for fifteen artists to visit Israel. Working from dawn to dusk, they spent eight days touring and four days in Jerusalem and the results of their labours were brought together for a special exhibition 'Israel at 50 – Artistic Impressions'.

The Llewelyn Alexander Gallery mentioned in the article above is directly opposite the Old Vic in Lambeth and Ken's paintings would look out at the theatre where, all those years ago, his mother had danced to entertain the crowds waiting to go in.

Ken with sketchbook in Israel

Ken rented a studio on the river Thames on Platts Eyot. The studio gave both he and Debra space to work and the environment was beautiful and relaxed. I mentioned briefly the strange, eclectic mix of people and businesses that were housed on the island, well they worked. A group of misfits and dreamers all enjoying their privileged home. Ken was popular with the fellow islanders and they enjoyed having him amongst them and his students, who would brighten up the surrounds. These students would come for the day and they would all work together, sometimes with models and sometimes from the surrounding scenery. He would teach and laugh and it was a halcyon period of his life. Some lifelong friendships were made.

From there he was approached by a producer and a film was made 'Ken Paine – Painting Faces' for Sky TV. On this particular film, Ken paints the actor Joss Ackland and it is a thoroughly enjoyable programme, showing him teaching and talking and ultimately painting the portrait.

But, as they say, good things never last. Ken has a favourite saying … 'put a mark where your happiness is because it won't be there tomorrow'. Debra, who had been making a name for herself in the art world and was leading an increasingly busy life, died. Suddenly, prematurely and shockingly, in 2002 at the age of 41, of a heart attack. Ken was shattered. He let the studio go and found himself once again on his own.

'Tittle Tattle'

'The Veteran'

'There is only one success -
to be able to spend your life in your own way'

Two years later I met him.

I met him at one of his courses at Dedham Hall. I knew nothing of his past. I knew nothing of Debra and the tragedy he had been through. I had two grown up sons of my own and was at the end of a 32 year marriage. We continued to meet after the course finished and, by the end of the same year, some eight months after I first met him, I moved into his life for good. We have been together now for ten years and I have learned so much from him, both about painting and about life. We paint together most days, although his influence is so strong that I paint upstairs and he paints downstairs. But even so, he tends to dictate my mood by his choice of music. Music is such an essential part of his painting that I wouldn't presume to interfere ... well, sometimes I might. Mostly I just shut the door.

Today Ken's reputation and talent brings students to his door. They are in awe of him. They arrive at his cottage/studio and step over the threshold into his wonderland. The house is festooned with art. Art in frames, art on paper, unfinished art, art in progress on the easel. Mirrors and snippets cut from newspapers and magazines, quotations and an eclectic mix of anything that has taken his fancy.

Living space is irrelevant and very much takes second place to the painting

On one occasion, when Ken was invited to talk to the Richmond Art Society, of which he is the President, he arrived to a maximum audience amongst which was a young American student who had flown over from Florence where he was studying, to meet Ken Paine. He had picked up the notice of Ken's lecture on the Internet and was anxious to meet the artist he was spending his time trying to emulate. Ever eager to meet and encourage new talent, Ken invited him over to spend the day with us.

The young man rang up early the next morning to say he had found his way over to Hampton Court station. Back he came and had some breakfast and coffee whilst hanging on Ken's every word. They chatted and looked at paintings all morning and Ken suggested they drive over to Bushy Park to have a walk in the sunshine before he went back to London.

There are several lifetimes between 20 years and 85 years and certainly completely different lives. Ken took the young man to his car. An old, old, Ford

accent ... 'nobody's going believe this back home!'

We have continued to travel together; to Paris many times to support and exhibit at the annual shows of La Societe des Pastellistes de France; to Bordeaux where we met up with a great friend, the Countess Willimijn de Cazenove and her son, Louis. We visited her vineyard where we ate, drank and painted a glorious day away.

The French love Ken and they love his work. We were at a very special event in Paris run by the Societe des Pastellistes where he demonstrated to a large audience whilst being filmed, with the image appearing up on a large screen. He spoke to them in his pidgin French, which they loved, although mostly his words were translated. He demonstrated his remarkable talent and concluded by uncovering a new sheet of paper and writing the word FIN. I remember the audience and fellow master pastellistes rose to their feet, as one. A DVD was made of the event with five Master Pastellistes (including Ken) demonstrating their art.

Another DVD was made some time after that, which again meant a trip to Paris for Ken and myself. We were hosted by a lovely lady, Claire, who also undertook the job of translating on the film. The producer was a rather bombastic (perhaps chauvinistic) Frenchman but he had found a model with a very interesting face and Ken duly did his stuff. It was an unusual experience. To keep me quiet, the producer handed me a camera to take some film of the film being made. Very generously he added my name to the credits.

In 2009, we went to India with another very dear friend, Mahesh Patel, who showed us different aspects of the country in Mumbai and Varanasi and welcomed us to his grandmother's village in sugar cane country. It was all fascinating and Mahesh's mother

Fiesta, badly dented, rusted and filthy both inside and out. As he hesitantly got in to the passenger seat, the young man looked in the back seat and asked .... if that was Ken's fender lying there? It was of course, having come off after a slight contretemps with a brick wall. Ken revved up the engine in his normal fashion and bounced along on his way to the park. But they ran out of petrol. One slight idiosyncrasy being that Ken would only ever put petrol in his car a 'fiver's worth' at a time. He uncovered a can with some petrol still in it but they had no funnel. The young American boy tried to fashion something from a rolled up magazine and, when that failed, a plastic bottle. They managed between them to get enough petrol into the tank to get to the park, leaving the boy almost hysterically crying in his American

'Mahesh's Grandmother'

'Maude'

142

and aunt hosted our time in the village. We were treated to home cooked local produce that was utterly delicious. Quite what the local people made of Ken is unrecorded but we were made very welcome. Throughout our trip, Ken would look and watch and sometimes sketch the people surrounding him. In truth, he found the peace and tranquility of the village difficult to cope with but he loved the hustle and bustle of life in Varanasi. Basically he was born and remains 'a city boy'.

Ken had a large exhibition of his work at the Frost & Reed Gallery in London. It was during their 200th anniversary year and the exhibition was co-ordinated by Managing Director, John Molony - a charming man, who wrote the following:

'Ken's capacity to make each of his subjects wholly original, wholly them-selves, is a massive affirmation of the value of life. There are no tricks, no parody, no condescension, no beauti-fying ... they are among the most truthful paintings I have ever seen and, because it is Ken who is telling the truth, the truth has become beautiful.'

There was also his wonderful 80th birthday party at the Arts Club in Dover Street. Music is vital to Ken and his painting. At that party, the guests were welcomed by the gentle music of a pianist whilst they drank their cham-pagne and ate their canapes. Down-stairs, where we later retired, a film show of his paintings was shown to the music of Billie Holiday before Ken chatted to the audience - his friends. The event raised a significant amount of money for charity and was so lovely, largely due to the time and effort and love put into it by Linda Blackstone and the help and advice of Sir Alex Reed.

The exhibition at l'Abbaye de Flaran that I mentioned previously, was another fabulous excuse for a party. Michael Simonow entertained us royally and many, many of Ken's friends, family and supporters travelled over to view the paintings on show. We stayed for several days and, apart from spending so much valued time with Michael and his wife Astrid, we enjoyed a lunch party on the banks of the river La Baise. It was exactly like something out of the Impressionist era. There we were, an eclectic mix of artists and friends and family, on a sunny day by the river, drinking and eating on rustic tables and sitting on plastic chairs. It just was such a special time.

The following was posted on the internet:

'The summer promises once again to be rich in sensory pleasures at the Abbaye d'Flaran that welcomes the beginning of the summer season of new works of rare quality. The exhibition not to be missed is undoubtedly that of the contemporary painter Ken Paine, opened today in the presence of the artist himself. Excerpted from the series 'Portrait' by Simonow presented last year, his paintings are part of this same theme, which the artist has focused his work since the 1980s' **Justine Mesnard of La Depeche.Fr.**

I have accompanied Ken to all his teaching venues and demonstrations and witnessed the fun, the laughter and friendship that he inspires wherever he goes.

At home ... we paint.

'Florrie'

'Flower'

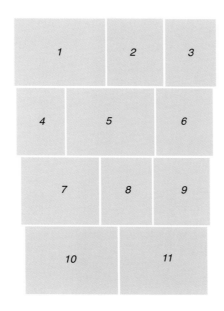